CONTENTS

Words in **bold** are explained in the glossary.

Fun at the zoo

It's Sunday.

We are going to the **zoo**!

I love reading

Editorial consultant: Mitch Cronick

Tick

Look at the zoo **map**.

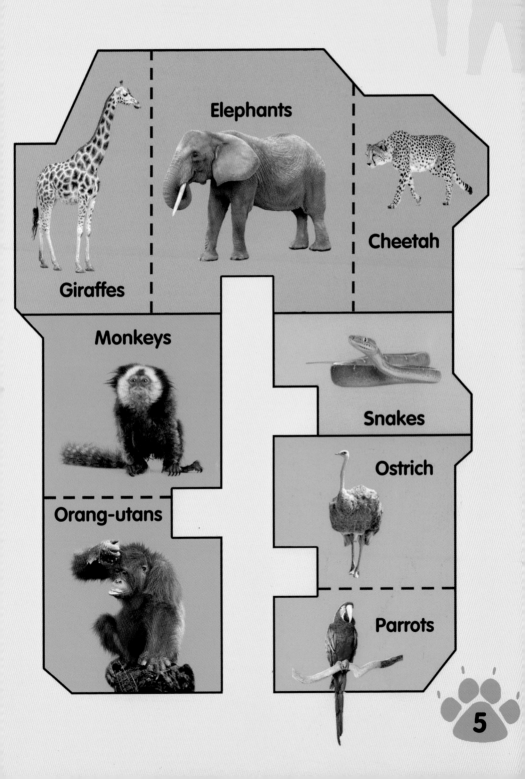

Elephants

Cheetah

Giraffes

Monkeys

Snakes

Ostrich

Orang-utans

Parrots

Tall giraffes

Giraffes are the tallest animals in the world.

Look at the cheetah

Cheetahs are the fastest
animals in the world.

Big elephants

Elephants are the biggest animals that live on land.

11

Look at the monkeys

Monkeys love to climb.

Monkeys like to swing.

Time for lunch

The orang-utan eats his lunch.

Orang-utan lunch

Apple

Orange

Banana

Carrots

Broccoli

15

Peek at the parrots

The parrots have red, blue and yellow feathers.

Feathers

Look at the ostrich

The ostrich lays the biggest egg in the world!

Ostrich egg

Chicken egg

19

Meet a snake

The **zookeeper** holds a snake.

Snake

It is long and green.

Zookeeper

Glossary

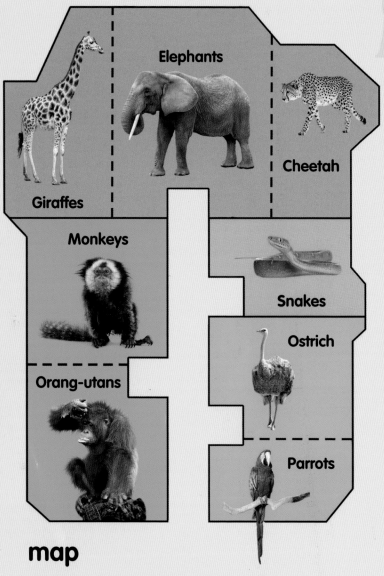

Elephants

Cheetah

Giraffes

Monkeys

Snakes

Ostrich

Orang-utans

Parrots

map

A drawing of a place that helps us to find things and find our way around.

zoo

A place where lots of different wild animals live. We can go to the zoo to see the animals and learn about them.

zookeeper

A person who cares for the animals in a zoo.

Index

An Hachette UK Company
www.hachette.co.uk
Copyright © Octopus Publishing Group Ltd 2013
First published in Great Britain in 2010 by TickTock, an imprint of Octopus Publishing Group Ltd,
Endeavour House, 189 Shaftesbury Avenue, London WC2H 8JY.
www.octopusbooks.co.uk

ISBN 978 1 84898 231 4

Printed in China
1 3 5 7 9 10 8 6 4 2

Picture credits (t=top, b=bottom, c=centre, l=left, r=right, OFC=outside front cover, OBC=outside back cover):
Digital Vision (RF Disc): 5bl, 22bl. Image Source/Getty Images: 20–21, 23b. iStock: 1, 7, 14, 23t.
NHPA/Adrian Hepworth: 13. Shutterstock: OFC, Flap, 2, 4, 5tr, 5tc, 5tl, 5cr (both), 5cl, 5br, 6, 8–9, 12, 15 (all), 16–17,
18, 19, 22tr, 22tc, 22tl, 22cr (both), 22cl, 22cr, OBC. vario images GmbH & Co.KG/Alamy: 10.